Packets of Sunlight For Parents

Compiled by Marnie L. Pehrson

If you enjoy this book, you'll also enjoy
Packets of Sunlight for American Patriots
http://www.SheLovesGod.com/packets

© 2002 Marnie L. Pehrson. All Rights Reserved.
Published by C.E.S. Business Consultants
Tel: 706-866-2295 * webmaster@SheLovesGod.com
http://www.SheLovesGod.com/packets

Artwork from Microsoft Clipart Gallery

ISBN 0-9676162-4-7

Preface

Richard G. Scott once said that the Lord, "will place in your path *packets of spiritual sunlight to brighten your way.* They often come after the trial has been the greatest, as evidence of the compassion and love of an all-knowing Father. They point the way to greater happiness, more understanding, and strengthen your determination to accept and be obedient to His will. (Richard G. Scott "Trust in the Lord" November 1994 *Ensign*, p.17)

Every parent has times when he or she doubts his or her ability to raise children, to be a good parent, or to just survive the challenges of the day. We each need packets of spiritual sunlight to brighten our way. This book is a collection of quotations and advice for parents that do just that.

I began this collection as a way to bolster myself as a busy mother of six and in the process found gems of wisdom that I wanted to share with others.

I hope you enjoy!

Marnie L. Pehrson

Motherhood –
The Greatest Potential for Good

"Motherhood is the greatest potential influence either for good or ill in human life. The mother's image is the first that stamps itself on the unwritten page of the young child's mind. It is her caress that first awakens a sense of security, her kiss, the first realization of affection; her sympathy and tenderness, the first assurance that there is love in the world.... Motherhood consists of three principle attributes or qualities: namely a) the power to bear, 2) the ability to rear, 3) the gift of love... This ability and willingness properly to rear children, the gift to love, and eagerness, yes, longing to express it in soul development, make motherhood the noblest office or calling in the world. She who can paint a masterpiece or write a book that will influence millions deserves the admiration and the plaudits of mankind; but she who rears successfully a family of healthy, beautiful sons and daughters, whose influence will be felt through generations to come... deserves the highest honor that man can give and the choicest blessings of God." (David O. McKay, Gospel Ideals, p. 452-454)

"Lo, children are an heritage of the Lord. As arrows are in the hand of a mighty man; so are children of the youth. Happy is the man that hath his quiver full of them. "

- Psalms 127:3-5

a quiver full

The Little People
John Greenleaf Whittier

A dreary place would be this earth,
Were there no little people in it;
The song of life would lose its mirth,
Where there no children to begin it.

No little forms, like buds to grow,
And make the admiring heart surrender;
No little hands on breasts and brow,
To keep the thrilling love-chords tender.

The sterner souls would grow more stern,
Unfeeling nature more inhuman,
And man to stoic coldness turn,
And woman would be less than woman.

Life's song, indeed, would lose its charm,
Were there no babies to begin it;
A doleful place this world would be,
Were there no little people in it.

A Mother's Influence Burns Upon the Character of Her Children

"As I look back over my life and the influence that my mother had on me, I realize that the things she taught me have never left my memory. They are burned into my character and will stay there forever. A righteous mother's influence for good spans the generations and touches the lives of so many more than her own children. Her influence radiates in the lives of her children, her grandchildren and great-grandchildren and out to all they come in contact." (Marnie Pehrson)

spans generations

Work on Your Marriage

"If you are married, plan a 'date night' with your spouse. It is too easy to lose the romance in a marriage over the years. Take one night a week or at least every other week to spend with your spouse. You do not have to do anything expensive. Be creative and do things you both enjoy. Find the things that made you fall in love in the first place, and keep them alive. When a father and mother love each other, the children can sense it. It gives them more security in their lives when home is an enjoyable place to be. " (Marnie Pehrson)

enjoy a date night

The Essence of Womanhood

"Motherhood is more than bearing children, though it is certainly that. It is the essence of who we are as women. It defines our very identity, our divine stature and nature, and the unique traits our Father gave us." (Sheri L. Dew, "Are We Not All Mothers?" *Ensign,* Nov. 2001, 96)

divine stature

Do a 180

"Parents who find themselves participating in negative interactions with their children, whether they started it or not, can reverse this trend by 'doing a 180.' Another way of saying this is 'do the opposite' of what parents are currently doing and not finding very effective. If, for instance, the parent discovers that they raise their voice with a particular child over a specific issue during a particular time of the day, then that parent can try 'doing a 180.' Instead they can strive to lower their voice, change the issue, or discuss it at a different time of day. Or, if a parent finds that they tend to be more tired and grumpy at the end of the day or their child more moody in the morning, try reducing the overall interaction with that person during that time.

"Use humor by putting up a storm warning sign on the refrigerator or a grumpy person crossing sign in the hallway. Parents can try doing the opposite

reverse the trend

of what they would normally do in a given situation and break the stronghold that the negative scripts have on the family. 'Doing a 180' introduces a novel stimulus to a negative situation and thereby reverse its negative course." (Ron Huxley, LMFT, "The Most Important Role of Your Life," www.parentingtoolbox.com)

No Greater Obligation

"I remind mothers everywhere of the sanctity of your calling. No other can adequately take your place. No responsibility is greater, no obligation more binding than that you rear in love and peace and integrity those whom you have brought into the world." (Gordon B. Hinckley, "Bring Up a Child in the Way He Should Go," *Ensign*, Nov. 1993, 54)

sanctity of calling

What's Negotiable?

"The first step in teaching values to children is to decide what is negotiable from what is not negotiable. Some parents will not allow any discussion on observances, rules, and conduct while other parents allow their child freedom to decide. In some families, religious observance may or may not be negotiable. Going to church or observing religious ceremonies may not be an option, at least when the children are young. Other nonnegotiable values may involve family rules, for example when expressing anger. Parents may decide that family members are not allowed "to hurt themselves, other people, or property." When angry, children may throw a tantrum, involving biting themselves, hitting their parents, or breaking toys and furniture. Very strict parents feel threatened by a child's expression of anger while other parents allow it to go unchecked. A more balanced parenting approach would be to accept the anger but not its destructive, uncontrolled venting.

set boundaries

This gives parent's self-permission to intervene when necessary. Other examples of what is nonnegotiable might include: 'No misuse or abuse of drugs or alcohol,' 'no R or X-rated movies', or 'no more than one friend in the car at a time when driving to and from school.'

"One way that parents get stuck when deciding on what is negotiable or nonnegotiable is holding opposite beliefs about attending church or expressing anger. When one parent wants to take children to church, the other parent may have strong feelings of opposition to it. One parent may be comfortable with a child's tantrum, and not bothered by it, while another parent cannot tolerate the kicking and screaming. When parents disagree, children 'divide and conquer.' It is important that parents find a middle ground and have open lines of communication with each other if they are to effectively teach values to their children." (Ron Huxley, LMFT, "Four Steps to Teaching Children Values," www.parentingtoolbox.com)

A Spirit of Service

"We love those whom we
serve. If the relationship
with your husband is
strained, serve him. Perform
at least one act of service for
him – something he can't or won't
do for himself – each day. Look for ways
you can make him happy and soon you
will rediscover your love for each other.

"Teach your children to serve one
another and in doing so, they will learn to
love one another. I have noticed that when
I positively praise or reward my children
for the good that they do and try not to
dwell on their mistakes, we all get along
better, and they are more likely to continue
to be helpful in the home. " (Marnie
Pehrson)

love follows service

Teach Values by Example

"Another way to teach values to children is "to participate in community events and services that support parent's beliefs. This might include volunteering at a senior center, delivering meals to shut-in's, or attending a rally on child abuse. A sense of community can help to create a feeling of identity, as a family and as an individual. Children are already listening to the values broadcasted on the Internet, television, and radio and are making choices based on what they see and hear. Parents can take a more active role by aligning their children to what parents believe are more positive values by participating in community events that support those values.

"Parents might get stuck on this step by a lack of resources or programs to involve themselves in, in their area. If this is the case, parents can create a program of their own. Talk to businesses and organizations in the area for support and demonstrate to children how to take a leadership role in community issues and problems. This will be more powerful on children's psyches than volunteering." (Ron Huxley, LMFT, "Four Steps to Teaching Children Values", www.parentingtoolbox.com)

When You're Overwhelmed

"Slow down and focus on God. Learn to say NO to over-volunteerism. Rather than being intimidated by the Proverbs 31 woman, be inspired. Let this serve as motivation to be all you can be for your husband, yourself, your children, and your God. Lower your expectations, not your standards." (Debbie Williams, Author/ Speaker, www.OrganizedTimes.com)

focus on God

Teach Love of Country and Freedom

"My father is a true patriot, a friend to freedom. He taught us to love and understand the Constitution of the United States and instilled in us the ability to determine which laws or candidates were constitutionally sound and those that were not. He sees freedom as our most treasured gift from God, and taught us that freedom is protected and fostered when we make right choices and give other people that same freedom. We cannot build our own freedom by taking away the freedom of another individual. Take time to study the laws of your country and build a love of country in your home." (Marnie Pehrson)

a treasured gift

Build a Spiritual Inheritance

"A bumper sticker on the back of an expensive recreational vehicle read: 'We're spending our children's inheritance.' While many parents strive to save wealth and property to hand down to their children, how many parents will make an effort to leave a spiritual inheritance for them?

"In the introduction to her book *10 Principles for Spiritual Parenting*, Mimi Doe writes: 'Children are spiritual beings.' She considers a child's spirituality to be innate but that parents and other adults 'clobber it out of them.' Parents who want to develop moral and ethical behavior in children must nurture these qualities in their child. One of reasons parents 'clobber' or discourage these qualities in children is that they are not attuned with their own spirituality.

"Parents are psychological and spiritual mirrors to children. 'Children form their earliest ideas about God, the world, people, and trust from what is mirrored from you,' says Doe.

innate spirituality

"How do you act, or react, to circumstances? Do you scream at the guy who just cut you off on the road? Do you make fun of other people? Do you tantrum when you are frustrated? A child's identity is filtered through the beliefs and behaviors of their parent. "

"Doe suggests that parents let go of people or situations that drag them and the children down, physically and spiritually. When you are around exciting and stimulating people whom love life, you feel excited and full of life too, right? But when you are around people and situations that deplete the emotional reserves, you feel negative and empty.

"The same is true for children. They need vibrant, spiritual parents who give them life. And, they need parents to make tough decisions about where they should go, what they should watch, and who they should socialize with to help them develop their spiritual and moral selves. If this is done early in a child's life, they will have a better chance later in life, to act morally and know the value of their own spirituality. A proverb, in the Holy Bible, says, 'Train a child when he is young and

when he is old, he will not depart from it.'
Sound investment tips there!" (Ron Huxley,
LMFT, *Moral Development of Children:
Spiritual Inheritance,*
www.parentingtoolbox.com)

Mothers, Do You Know?

"Here's a beautiful tribute by a son to his mother: 'I don't remember much about her views of voting nor her social prestige; and what her ideas on child training, diet, and eugenics were, I cannot recall. The main thing that sifts back to me now through the thick undergrowth of years is that she loved me. She liked to lie on the grass with me and tell stories, or to run and hide with us children. She was always hugging me. And I liked it. She had a sunny face. To me it was like God, and all the beatitudes saints tell of Him. And sing! Of all the sensations pleasurable to my life nothing can compare with the rapture of crawling up into her lap and going to sleep while she swung to and fro in her rocking chair and sang. Thinking of this, I wonder if the woman of today, with all her tremendous notions and plans, realizes what an almighty factor she is in shaping of her child for weal or woe. I wonder if she realizes how much sheer love and attention count for in a child's life.' " (Ezra Taft Benson, Fireside for parents, 22, Feb. 1987)

Making Spiritual Investments

"Most financial advisors show the need to start investing early in life. They love to demonstrate how a small, monthly investment, over the long haul, reaps greater financial rewards over large investments later in life. Spiritually, parents need to invest early and consistently, in small ways. But parents can start late too. In the moral and spiritual market, late can be almost as good as early, to invest. " (Ron Huxley, LMFT, *Moral Development of Children: Spiritual Inheritance,* www.parentingtoolbox.com)

Set Aside Your Differences

"It is useless to debate which parent is most important. No one would doubt that a mother's influence is paramount with newborns in the first years of a child's life. The father's influence increases as the child grows older. However, each parent is necessary at various times in a child's development. Both fathers and mothers do many intrinsically different things for their children. Both mothers and fathers are equipped to nurture children, but their approaches are different. Mothers seem to take a dominant role in preparing children to live within their families (present and future). Fathers seem best equipped to prepare children to function in the environment outside the family. . . .

"Parents in any marital situation have a duty to set aside personal differences and encourage each other's righteous influence in the lives of their children." (James E. Faust, "Father, Come Home," *Ensign*, May 1993, 35)

each is necessary

Set Rules and Expectations

"Contrary to what they would have you believe, children like rules. Of course they would never admit it, but children feel more security and love when rules are in place. When rules are set and followed consistently, children know what to expect. For example, if Johnny knows that if he yells and screams while you are on the phone, he will be sent to his room for five minutes, he'll learn not to yell and scream. (That is if his room is not an extremely fun place.) Perhaps a corner may be better? Yet, if 50% of the time you do nothing with Johnny when he yells and screams, and the other 50% you send him to the corner, he learns to take his chances.

"The hardest thing to me with children is being consistent. Consistency is especially difficult when you run a business from home. You are so busy that you overlook things. You let things slide. In the process, your children learn the most opportune times to get away with things. They especially know how to take advantage of your busiest times. They know Mommy or Daddy will not hang up on that important call to send them to their room. So that is when they will hit their younger siblings, yell, scream, and climb in the kitchen cabinets. You may think I'm saying that children are devious and manipulative. I'm not saying that so much as I'm saying that they are smart little human beings with natural tendencies. It is human nature to try to get away with what we can, unless we have some firm morale background that dictates otherwise.

"This is how rules help. Rules provide a firm moral background for children. When rewards for obeying rules and punishments for disobeying them are offered consistently, children feel more secure. They know that their parents love them and care about them. They may not always like the rules, but they will learn to respect your rules and love you more for it over time.

"If you have children and teens, you may be better off setting fewer 'little rules' and being more consistent in enforcing and rewarding the more important ones. You must be the judge in your own family, but remember consistency is the key." (Marnie Pehrson)

Little versus Big Talks

"Most parents feel they must go through the anxiety of having the big talk when it comes to subjects like sex and drugs. Does anyone really enjoy the big talk or learn any life values from it? It may be more effective to have lots of little talks instead. Those golden moments behind beer delivery trucks are one example. During the television commercials might be another. Talking is not a one-way conversation either. That's for the big talks. In the big talks, you get it out and over with as soon as possible. Slap the dust off your hands and pat your own back for a parenting job well done. No, for the little talks, you have to listen. Make it a dialogue, not just a monologue. On the way to the mall, ask them their thoughts about why a sexy woman was displayed next to a bottle of alcohol, on that billboard on the side of the road. Start a conversation, on the way home from the

doctor's visit, on the differences between legal and illegal drugs. Do you know the difference? Those little talks vaccinate your child. They are little shots of conversation on the dangers of substance abuse that inoculate your child against chemical disease." (Ron Huxley, LMFT, "Finding Your Voice: Talking to Your Children About Drugs and Alcohol," www.parentingtoolbox.com)

When Children Stray

"Perhaps there is no mother or father who hasn't said, 'May the Lord help me to live "twenty-five" hours every day to dedicate my life to motherhood and fatherhood so that no child of mine can ever rightly say that I didn't do everything in my power to persuade him to desist.' Some of our children remain firm and true, and yet others begin to stray away, and sometimes we don't understand why. But may we all resolve that as parents today we will live close to our children, we will counsel with them, we will give them the foundation of rock-bottom principles of divine truth, except for which they will be like a ship without a rudder and without an anchor in times of storm and stress that are sure to blow and beat upon every one of them." (Harold B. Lee, Funeral Services for Carol Anniett Clayton, Salt Lake City, February 1963; see *The Teachings of Harold B. Lee* p. 276.)

an anchor

The characteristics Paul used to describe a bishop apply equally to fathers. He wrote that a bishop should be "one that ruleth well his own house, having his children in subjection with all gravity: (For if a man know not how to rule his own house, how shall he take care of the Church of God?)"

- 1 Timothy 3:4-5

The Value of Work

"The foundation of self-reliance is hard work. Parents should teach their children that work is the prerequisite to achievement and success in every worthwhile endeavor. Children of legal age should secure productive employment and begin to move away from dependence on parents. None of us should expect others to provide for us that which we can provide for ourselves." (Joseph B. Wirthlin, "Fruits of the Gospel of Jesus Christ," General Conference Oct. 1991; see *Ensign*, Nov. 1991, p. 16)

self-reliance

Work With Your Children

"My mother was always working. I'm not talking about a career really, although she did have a good career before marrying my father and having children with him. She was always working. She was cleaning, cooking, planting flowers, working in the yard, or teaching us to do the same. We had regular jobs that we had to do. She taught us that being part of a family meant everyone chipped in — not just the mother slaving thanklessly while no one else lifted a finger. She got in there with us and showed us how to work, taught us the proper way to vacuum, to dust, to mop, to wash dishes. She instilled an intense desire to work for what we wanted in life. And as a result, all of her children are hardworking, resourceful individuals." (Marnie Pehrson)

work together

Gloomy? Reach Out to Others

"We have been sent into the world to do good to others; and in doing good to others we do good to ourselves. We should always keep this in view, the husband in reference to his wife, the wife in reference to her husband, the children in reference to their parents, and the parents in reference to their children. There is always opportunity to do good to one another. When you find yourselves a little gloomy, look around you and find somebody that is in a worse plight than yourself; go to him and find out what the trouble is, then try to remove it with the wisdom which the Lord bestows upon you; and the first thing you know, your gloom is gone, you feel light, the Spirit of the Lord is upon you, and everything seems illuminated." (Lorenzo Snow, 6 April 1899, CR, pp. 2-3)

opportunity for good

Pray Together

"I know of no single practice that will have a more salutary effect upon your lives than the practice of kneeling together as you begin and close each day. Somehow the little storms that seem to afflict every marriage are dissipated when, kneeling before the Lord, you thank him for one another, in the presence of one another, and then together invoke his blessings upon your lives, your home, your loved ones, and your dreams.

   "God then will be your partner, and your daily conversations with him will bring peace into your hearts and a joy into your lives that can come from no other source. Your companionship will sweeten through the years; your love will

God as your partner

strengthen. Your appreciation for one
another will grow.

"Your children will know the security of
a home where dwells the Spirit of the Lord.
You will gather them together in that
home... and teach them in love. They will
know parents who respect one another, and
a spirit of respect will grow in their hearts.
They will experience the security of the
kind word softly spoken, and the tempests
of their own lives will be stilled. They will
know a father and mother who, living
honestly with God, live honestly also with
one another and with their fellowmen.
They will grow up with a sense of
appreciation, having heard their parents in
prayer express gratitude for blessings great
and small. They will mature with faith in
the living God.

The destroying angel of domestic
bitterness will pass you by and you will know
peace and love throughout your lives which
may be extended into all eternity. I could
wish for you no greater blessing." (Gordon
B. Hinckley, "Except the Lord Build the
House," *Ensign*, June 1971, p. 72)

"Train up a child in the way he should go: and when he is old, he will not depart from it"

- Proverbs 22:6

Building Self Esteem of Each Family Member

"When you are busy with the details of life, some people will naturally get lost in the shuffle. Do not let those people be your family. I have six children, each with totally different personalities. My oldest daughter is 'the boss.' She demands attention, and usually gets it. My second son 'demands' attention in his own sweet way. He gives me a hug or a kiss. He knows just how to ask for things, 'We could make cookies!' he positively questions with a sweet grin. His advances are irresistible. But, my oldest son, is not so demanding in his requests for attention. Because of this, in the past I feel I have let him be lost in the hurry. He's a very good boy who does not demand much or trouble much. He's my easiest one, yet I sometimes reward him the least, because I am so busy. This is a prime example of ignoring a family member's needs.

a feeling of worth

"Each member of our family needs to feel of worth. Our spouses need to be encouraged in their careers, and our children need us to go to their sporting events and recitals. They need us to praise them in front of other people while they are within earshot. These things build their self-esteem. Most importantly, they need our time and attention. They need us to listen. " (Marnie Pehrson)

Educating Desires

"It is very gratifying to parents to be able to respond to the desires of their children, but it is undoubtedly a cruelty to a child to give it everything it asks for. Children may wisely be denied things which even in themselves are harmless. Our pleasures depend often more upon the qualities of our desires than upon the gratification. A child may be ladened with gifts which afford him little or no pleasure, simply because he has no desire for them. The education then of our desires is one of far-reaching importance to our happiness in life; and when we learn that there is an education of our intellects and we are set about that education with prudence and wisdom, we shall do much to increase not only our happiness but also our usefulness in the world." (Joseph F. Smith, *Gospel Doctrine*, p. 297)

happiness in life

Caring for Souls

"Our Heavenly Father placed the responsibility upon parents to see that their children are well fed, well groomed and clothed, well trained, and well taught. Most parents protect their children with shelter — they tend and care for their diseases, provide clothes for their safety and their comfort, and supply food for their health and growth. But what do they do for their souls?" *(The Teachings of Spencer W. Kimball,* ed. Edward L. Kimball [1982], 332).

"I looked on my right hand, and beheld, but there was no man that would know me: refuge failed me; no man cared for my soul" (Psalms 142:4).

"Several years ago I was working in my garden and was delighted to see a family of quail. I watched the father sitting on top of the wall standing guard. The mother was busy keeping her 10 precious babies together and seemed to be demonstrating how to peck in the earth for food. I was

subtle dangers

fascinated. I carefully and quietly walked closer. All too soon I was detected by the watchful father, and he let out a warning call. The mother tried to guide the children around the wall to safety, but I — the danger — was too near, and she became frustrated and confused and flew up on the wall by the father. I didn't want to harm this family, so I quickly retreated out of sight.

"Unlike my experience with the quail family, the dangers threatening the lives of our families do not retreat. Satan rejoices in our confusion and frustration, and his influences surround us. We turn on the television — is this a family show? We hear something coming out of our child's room — is this music? We try to pick a movie — did this one really have an acceptable rating?

"Sometimes Satan's influences are more subtle. I have asked myself these questions: Do I leave my children exposed to danger when I don't teach them the truths of the gospel? Do I neglect their souls when I don't help them recognize the promptings of the Spirit and the guidance they can receive? Do I leave my children exposed to danger when my example is not the same as my words or when I don't share my love in such a way that each child feels it deeply?" (Patricia P. Pinegar, "Caring for the Souls of Children," *Ensign*, May 1997, 13)

Eli ministered faithfully in his calling as a priest but apparently neglected his family. When his children followed after wickedness, the Lord said: "… I will perform against Eli all things which I have spoken concerning his house. … For I have told him that I will judge his house for ever for the iniquity which he knoweth; because his sons made themselves vile, and he restrained them not."

- 1 Samuel 3:12-13

Using Time Wisely

"My mother taught us to use our time wisely. We learned quickly that you don't tell Moma that you're bored. If you did, you'd quickly be given some household chores to enliven your day. If we fought or quarreled, we were put to work. My mother lived by the motto that an 'idle mind is the devil's workshop.' Constructive use of time was paramount, and that principle is indelibly burned into the character of her children." (Marnie Pehrson)

put to work

Control Your Temper and Voice

"Never forget that these little ones are the sons and daughters of God and that yours is a custodial relationship to them, that He was a parent before you were parents and that He has not relinquished His parental rights or interest in these little ones. Now, love them, take care of them. Fathers, control your tempers, now and in all the years to come. Mothers, control your voices, keep them down. Rear your children in love, in the nurture and admonition of the Lord. Take care of your little ones, welcome them into your homes and nurture and love them with all of your hearts." (Gordon B. Hinckley, Salt Lake University Third Stake conference, 3 Nov. 1996; in Church News, 1 Mar. 1997, 2).

children of God

"The fathers have eaten sour grapes, and the children's teeth are set on edge."

- Ezekiel 18:2

Set Family Goals That Are Achievable

"There are many types of families in this world. There are single parents, traditional families, and single people who live alone or with extended family. Yet, no matter the size or shape of your family, you need goals. People who work together toward a common goal and share common values learn greater love for each other, a spirit of teamwork, cooperation, and harmony. Without some common goals, each family member will wander in his or her own direction. This is what happens in many marriages where people married young, and then divorce in their 30's-40's because they do not have anything in common anymore. Each partner set their own goals, with no thought for their spouse. Although each spouse may have succeeded in their own goals, their directions were totally different. They became completely different people than when they first married. They maintained no common ground.

Do not let this happen to you and your family. Set goals together — even if those goals are not major. Even a small goal worked toward together will bring unity.

Some goals you could set as a family might be the following:

· Plan and save toward a vacation together;
· Clean out and remodel your basement as a family;
· A husband and wife could work and save for a new car;
· Select and hunt for a new home together;
· Work and set plans for your home business together;
· Work together to help a family member through a difficult school subject;
· Give quiet, study time to a parent who wants to go back to school.

Discover ways you can set goals in your own family. If you incorporate family nights for your family, you could use these nights to set goals, and work on family projects. Start with goals you know you can attain to build confidence. As you build a habit of goal-setting within your family, you can work toward more challenging goals. Always set goals that are attainable and worthwhile to all family members." (Marnie Pehrson)

We Shall Not Pass Again This Way

Richard L. Evans stated, We 'shall not pass again this way' and in these swift-passing scenes and seasons there seems to come insistently, almost above all else this compelling cry: Take time for your children. More and more, professional people are telling us that children are shaped and molded at a very early age" (Improvement Era, Nov. 1970, p. 125).

Home "is also the source of our personal lives, and in a sense the determiner of our everlasting lives. And so our plea is for parents to take the time it takes to draw near to the children God has given them. Let there be love at home. Let there be tenderness and teaching and caring for and not a shifting of responsibility onto others. God grant that we may never be too busy to do the things that matter most, for 'Home makes the man' " (Richard Evans' Quote Book, Salt Lake City: Publishers Press, 1971, p. 21).

take time for them

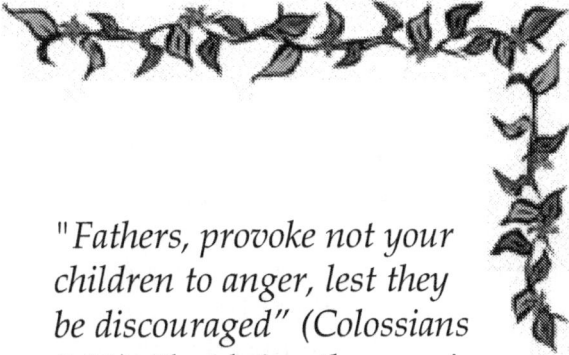

"Fathers, provoke not your children to anger, lest they be discouraged" (Colossians 3:21), "but bring them up in the nurture and admonition of the Lord" (Ephesians 6:4), for "the servant of the Lord must not strive; but be gentle ... , apt to teach, patient" (2 Timothy 2:24)

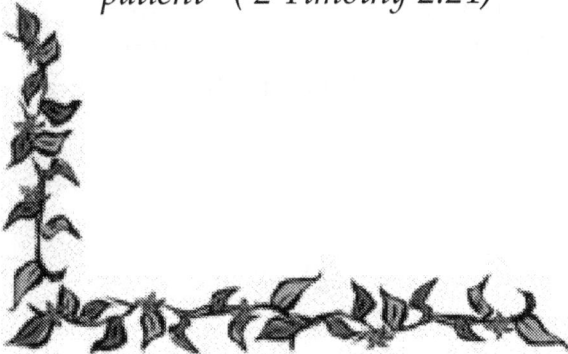

Fathers, Take Time to Teach

"Due to the level of family break-ups and divorce, more and more people today are being raised without the consistent influence of a good father. Many children are fortunate if they get to see their father every-other weekend. As I meet people who have grown up under these circumstances, my gratitude continues to grow for the fact that I had the blessed experience of being raised with my biological father not only in my home, but also as an active influence in my life.

"My fondest memories of childhood are those hours I spent sitting on the couch with my father as he taught me how to read and how to do math problems or just asked my opinion on things. Although my father has his flaws, just like any mortal man would, I don't think I could have had a better father. " (Marnie Pehrson)

fathers come home

Of Abraham, the Lord said: "For I know him, that he will command his children and his household after him, and they shall keep the way of the Lord. ..."

- Genesis 18:19.

Never Give Up Hope

"Perhaps few human challenges are greater than that of being good parents. Yes, even with the best intentions, conscientious, good parents sometimes experience feelings of despair, failure, and hurt when children do not make right choices and turn out the way we would like. Even in those circumstances it is so important for parents to love, pray for, and never give up hope for a son or daughter who may have strayed or brought disappointment." (Ben B. Banks, "Take Time for Your Children," *Ensign*, Nov. 1993, 28)

Keep Your Word

"My oldest sister fondly refers to our mother as, 'The burning bush.' If my mother said it would happen - regardless of whether it was punishment or reward - it would be carried out. 'So let it be written; so let it be done.' She didn't make promises she wasn't prepared to keep. If she promised you something, even if something else came up to intervene, she would still find a way to carry out her promises. In all my years of living, I can't recall that my mother ever told a single lie. Her character was and is beyond reproach." (Marnie Pehrson)

so let it be done

Bring Them Home

"The responsibilities of parenthood are of the greatest importance. The results of our efforts will have eternal consequences for us and the boys and girls we raise. Anyone who becomes a parent is under strict obligation to protect and love his children and assist them to return to their Heavenly Father" (Howard W. Hunter *Ensign*, Nov. 1983, p. 65).

eternal consequences

Nothing Can Replace Time and Affection

"My father spent hours with me teaching me, talking with me, and listening to me. It seemed as if we were inseparable. As a child I felt he belonged just to me because I got all the attention I needed.

"All those nights he spent tickling my belly, playing his harmonica or singing to me until I fell asleep are indelibly imprinted in my mind. As a child I felt incredibly loved, incredibly cared for. This foundation of affection built security, stability and trust in the most formative years of my life. Even at age 16, I remember my dad coming in my room when I had my friends over and he'd chat with us for a few minutes. As he'd leave I'd give him a kiss on his cheek. I remember one friend saying, 'You have such a great dad!' Even then, I knew I did. "
(Marnie Pehrson)

Discipline with Love

"'Discipline' and 'punishment' are not synonymous. Punishment suggests hurting, paying someone back for a wrong committed. Discipline implies an action directed toward a goal - of helping the recipient to improve himself" (William E. Homan, "How to Be a Better Parent," Reader's Digest, Oct. 1969, pp. 187-91).

goal of helping

Periodically Evaluate Family Strengths and Weaknesses

"Use your family nights to evaluate the progress you are making toward your goals. Use them as family councils to decide strategies and plans of actions for your family.

"Some families even go as far as to schedule 'interviews' with their children each month. They talk to each child about his school work, his challenges, and his friends. Of course, this should never be done in an interrogating way, but as one friend talking with another.

"Learn to find the hidden talents in others. Help your spouse and children see areas in which they are talented, and help them set goals toward progressing within those areas.

"It's also important to see the weaknesses in your children so that you can help them. For example, some children

family councils

are competitive and others are not. We should never force a noncompetitive child to participate in a highly-competitive sport against his/her will. Many parents try to live their lives through their children, and force them to relive their glory days. This may be fine with a child with an athletic talent, but can damage the esteem of one without.

"Learn to recognize the strengths and weaknesses of your spouse and children, and help them develop their God-given talents. This will not only help them build their self-esteem, but will also let them know just how much you love them. " (Marnie Pehrson)

Parenthood: A Sacred Trust

"Some worthy institutions have been developed to help improve the home and family life. But helpful as these agencies may be, I am convinced, and I believe you will agree, that there is not and never will be a better institution for improving the home than the home itself.

"Parents cannot, without regrettable consequences, shirk the responsibility of teaching and showing their children through their example the attributes of character that lead them unhesitatingly to appreciate and accept the good, the decent, the beautiful, and help them to develop the desire and the courage to turn from that which is coarse or crude or wrong.

"Parenthood is a sacred trust. It is an approach to the divine - a God-given privilege that, with its never-ending responsibilities, brings rich and lasting rewards." (ElRay L. Christiansen, "Successful Parenthood — A Noteworthy Accomplishment," *Ensign*, July 1972, 54)

no better institution

A Home Approved of God

"A home approved of God is not merely a place where children are born, but where their coming is received with joy and gladness by parents who strive with all their abilities to help their children develop such attributes as —

1. Faith in God, along with a desire to be obedient to his commandments,
2. Respect for and obedience to the laws of the land,
3. A determination to be truthful and honest, regardless of the circumstances,
4. Unselfishness by teaching (mostly by example), along with courtesy, respect, refinement, and good manners, for surely they are part of our religion.

After all,

"The sermon for a teenage child
That proves to be most ample
Is still the one that parents teach
By setting an example."
    - Hal Chadwick

received with joy

Success in family life calls for parents who take time to enjoy their children; who read with them; who play with them; who let them participate in planning special occasions, seeking to make wholesome family traditions a proud part of family life." (ElRay L. Christiansen, "Successful Parenthood-A Noteworthy Accomplishment," *Ensign*, July 1972, 54)

Rise Above Pettiness

"Another essential in successful parenthood is for fathers and mothers to avoid disputations. Such situations may seem harmless to the parents, but in the eyes of their children, the two most important people in the world are in conflict, and from their limited perspective, the whole world is in trouble. Situations thus created are an indication of immaturity and weakness on the part of those involved. Someone has said that one of the most important things a father can do for his children is to love and respect their mother.

"I plead with parents to rise above pettiness and to spare their children the inglorious and painful insecurity of having to endure petty disputations and offensive situations." (ElRay L. Christiansen, "Successful Parenthood-A Noteworthy Accomplishment," *Ensign*, July 1972, 54)

avoid disputations

No Nation Can Long Endure

"Historians almost without exception point out that one of the greatest contributing factors in the downfall of nations is the disintegration of the home and family life.

"A complete rebirth of satisfactory family life is needed. It is needed even in the so-called better homes. It must begin with proper love and respect between the husband and the wife and then, by their example, transferred to their children.

"No nation can long endure unless the great majority of its families and its homes are made secure through faith in God — an active, living faith." (ElRay L. Christiansen, "Successful Parenthood-A Noteworthy Accomplishment," *Ensign*, July 1972, 54)

secure through faith

Neglect Not the Fountain of Life

"We are guilty of many errors and many faults, but our worst crime is abandoning the children, neglecting the fountain of life. Many of the things we need can wait. The child cannot. Right now is the time his bones are being formed, his blood is being made, and his senses are being developed. To him we cannot answer tomorrow. His name is today." (Author Unknown)

children can't wait

Give Your Full Attention

"The parent who is overextended, who is burdened and distracted by too many other demands, simply cannot make time for many such routines and activities. We tend to direct things from a distance instead, sometimes even from a phone during business. 'Brush your teeth before you go to bed.' 'Don't forget to clean your room.' 'Be sure to practice a full half-hour.'

"Even when physically present, the overwhelmed parent often acts more like a drill sergeant than a loving mentor. Yet it is a parent's active and unhurried participation and dialogue that makes the difference. This contact must be interactive. Orders, lectures, and instructions are inadequate, as are questions that can be answered with "uh-huh," as in: 'Have you done your homework?' 'Uh-huh.' 'Did you have a good day at school?' 'Uh-huh.' 'Did you get that problem worked out?' 'Uh-huh.'

active & unhurried

"Meaningful interaction means dialogue, questions that help the child explore and make meaning out of his or her experiences. 'What was the most wonderful thing you saw today?' 'What will you do the next time you get angry with your brother?' 'What are your plans for bringing up your grade in English?' And it doesn't count if you are saying 'uh-huh' either, maybe while you listen and make dinner or watch the news at the same time. The important part of the dialogue is the listening: respectful, full-attention, eye-contact, putting-down-your-other-work listening, with encouraging nods and smiles and truly interested, respectful, and interactive comments."(Frances E. Warden, "Time and the Single Parent," *Ensign*, July 2000, 30)

You Are Not Alone

"I know of no single parent who has not experienced the long, dark night of the soul, feeling forsaken of the Spirit. Yet I am certain that we are never alone. Although we may not be aware of it, heaven is supporting us. Like Israel of old, we have God's promise that His kindness will not depart from us. No matter how dark it gets or how many other things pull at us, if we raise our children righteously, we will have succeeded. Some other dreams may go unachieved, other desires unfulfilled, and other goals unreached. Yet as with all sacrifices to the Lord, we will find that what we have gained is of immeasurably more worth than what we have given." (Frances E. Warden, "Time and the Single Parent," *Ensign*, July 2000, 30)

heaven's support

"For a small moment have I forsaken thee; but with great mercies will I gather thee."

"In a little wrath I hid my face from thee for a moment; but with everlasting kindness will I have mercy on thee, saith the Lord thy Redeemer. "

"For the mountains shall depart, and the hills be removed; but my kindness shall not depart from thee, neither shall the covenant of my peace be removed, saith the Lord that hath mercy on thee"

- Isaiah 54:7-8, 10

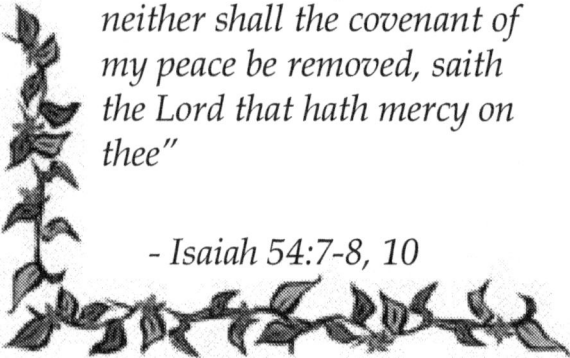

Secret to Happiness in Family Life

"The family is ordained of God. Marriage between man and woman is essential to His eternal plan. Children are entitled to birth within the bonds of matrimony, and to be reared by a father and a mother who honor marital vows with complete fidelity. Happiness in family life is most likely to be achieved when founded upon the teachings of the Lord Jesus Christ. Successful marriages and families are established and maintained on principles of faith, prayer, repentance, forgiveness, respect, love, compassion, work, and wholesome recreational activities. By divine design, fathers are to preside over their families in love and righteousness and are responsible to provide the necessities of life and protection for their families. Mothers are primarily responsible for the nurture of their children. In these sacred responsibilities, fathers and mothers are obligated to help one another as equal partners. Disability, death, or other circumstances may necessitate individual adaptation. Extended families should lend support when needed." ("The Family: A Proclamation to the World," *Liahona*, June 1996, 10)

The Greatest Trust

"It is said that 'to be trusted is a greater compliment than to be loved.' The greatest trust that can come to a man and woman is the placing in their keeping the life of a little child.

"If a man defaults who is entrusted with other people's funds — whether he be a bank, municipal, or state official—he is apprehended and probably sent to prison. If a person entrusted with a government secret discloses that secret and betrays his country, he is called a traitor.

"What must the Lord think, then, of parents who, through their own negligence or wilful desire to indulge their selfishness fail properly to rear their children, and thereby prove untrue to the greatest trust that has been given to human beings?" (David O. McKay, *Treasures of Life*, compiled by Clare Middlemiss, Deseret Book Company, 1965, p. 71.)

to be trusted

Home: Fundamental Institution

"In this age of selfishness and greed, of birth control and barrenness, of easy divorce, broken homes, and juvenile delinquency, in this age of cheap amusements, idleness and lack of discipline, it is well to search for basic values, to call attention to the fact that the home is the nation's most fundamental institution and that mothers are the first professors in that character-building school." (Hugh B. Brown, *Vision and Valor*, Bookcraft, 1971, p. 24.)

basic values

The First School, the First Church

"The home is where we
learn what is right, what
is good, and what is
kind. It is the first school
and the first church. The
best way to prepare a
child for a happy and
righteous adult life is to strengthen him
during his child life. And happy is the
family where this most important trust —
that of properly raising the children of that
family — is their greatest concern.

"Equal to the responsibility we have to
provide food and shelter and the necessities
of life is the responsibility to set the right
example for our children in all that we do.

"Let us remember that the parent in the
home influences the behavior patterns, the
habits, the opinions, and the beliefs of the
children. Most behavior patterns are
established early in life, and it is an
extremely difficult, slow task to change
them later in life." (O. Leslie Stone,
"Parenthood," *Ensign*, Nov. 1976, 60)

Five Things to Avoid

Among delinquent parents are these:

1. Those who quarrel in the presence of their children;

2. Those who pollute the home atmosphere with vulgarity and profanity;

3. Those whose daily home life does not conform to their Church pretensions;

4. Those who fail to teach obedience to their children;

5. Those who neglect to teach their children religion by saying, 'Let them grow up and choose for themselves,' thus failing in the discharge of a parental responsibility.

(David O. McKay, *Treasures of Life*, pp. 72-74.)

responsibility

Be Genuine

"Today our youth are faced with tremendous challenges — and what do they need most?

"They need sound knowledge, sensible understanding, a guiding hand. They need real homes that are maintained in a clean and orderly manner. They need fathers who are really fathers and mothers who are mothers in the true sense of the word. They need more than mere progenitors or landlords. They are in need of loving, understanding parents, who give fatherly and motherly care, who put their families first in their lives, and who consider it their fundamental and most important duty to save their own children, to so orient them and their thinking that they will not be swayed by every wind of persuasion which happens to blow in their direction.

"These young people are inquisitive, hungering for truth. What they want from us as parents is honest, well-informed answers to their questions, and our very lives should reflect the things we say, so that the teacher and the truth taught will be of the same pattern." (O. Leslie Stone, "Parenthood," *Ensign*, Nov. 1976, 60)

Instill a Love of Learning

"My Father spent many hours teaching me how to read and do math. As young as the age of 3, he had me reading the newspaper. He used to say he could give me anything to learn and I'd learn it – no questions asked. He said if he'd handed me a telephone book and said, 'Memorize this' I would have done it. I believe this is largely due to the love, confidence and trust I had in my father. Whatever he thought was worth learning, I knew must be worthwhile and even fun. These experiences built a foundation of love of learning that has continued throughout my life. It is one of the greatest gifts my father ever gave me." (Marnie Pehrson)

love learning

Working upon the Immortal Mind

Daniel Webster once said:

"If we work upon marble, it will perish. If we work upon brass, time will efface it. If we rear temples, they will crumble to dust. But if we work upon men's immortal minds, if we imbue them with high principles, with the just fear of God and love of their fellow men, we engrave on those tablets something which … will brighten and brighten to all eternity." (Burton Stevenson, *The Home Book of Quotations,* New York: Dodd, Mead & Company, 1934, p. 1312.)

time can't efface

*"Let your light so shine
before your [children], that
they may see your good
works, and glorify your
Father which is in heaven."*

- Matthew 5:16

"Paul delineated a parental pitfall when he commented that there were in the church "ten thousand instructors," but not many "fathers." (1 Cor. 4: 15.) The need, therefore, is not for parents who merely give facts, but for fathers who comfort and exhort "as a father doth his children." (1 Thes. 2:11.)" (Robert J. Matthews, "What the Scriptures Say about Rearing Children," *Ensign,* Dec. 1972, 34)

comfort & exhort

Build Confidence in Your Children

"My father actually raised me to be a bit of a show off and a ham-bone. He was so thrilled that I could read and do math tricks that he had me show them to everyone who came to the house. And of course, a young child is going to be on cloud nine when everyone starts ooh-ing and aah-ing over how smart she is. What confidence that built! To this day, I still have this compelling urge to take what I've learned and share it with others. And I largely attribute that level of confidence – the confidence to even *think* anything I'd have to say would be worthwhile to someone else – to my father's influence. So now you know who to blame for my verbosity. " (Marnie Pehrson)

share learning

With Parenthood Comes Responsibility

"Every individual in the world is a child of a mother and a father. Neither can ever escape the consequences of their parenthood. Inherent in the very act of creation is responsibility for the child who is created. None can with impunity run from that responsibility.

"It is not enough simply to provide food and shelter for the physical being. There is an equal responsibility to provide nourishment and direction to the spirit and the mind and the heart. Wrote Paul to Timothy, "But if any provide not for his own, and specially for those of his own house, he hath denied the faith, and is worse than an infidel" (1 Tim. 5:8).

"I am satisfied that Paul was speaking of more than physical nourishment." (Gordon B. Hinckley, "Bring Up a Child in the Way He Should Go," *Ensign*, Nov. 1993, 54)

nourish the spirit

So the Tree Is Bent

"Not long after we were married, we built our first home. We had very little money. I did much of the work myself. It would be called "sweat equity" today. The landscaping was entirely my responsibility. The first of many trees that I planted was a thornless honey locust. Envisioning the day when its filtered shade would assist in cooling the house in the summertime, I put it in a place at the corner where the wind from the canyon to the east blew the hardest. I dug a hole, put in the bare root, put soil around it, poured on water, and largely forgot it. It was only a wisp of a tree, perhaps three-quarters of an inch in diameter. It was so supple that I could bend it with ease in any direction. I paid little attention to it as the years passed.

"Then one winter day, when the tree was barren of leaves, I chanced to look out the window at it. I noticed that it was

start early

leaning to the west, misshapen and out of balance. I could scarcely believe it. I went out and braced myself against it as if to push it upright. But the trunk was now nearly a foot in diameter. My strength was as nothing against it. I took from my toolshed a block and tackle. Attaching one end to the tree and another to a well-set post, I pulled the rope. The pulleys moved a little, and the trunk of the tree trembled slightly. But that was all. It seemed to say, "You can't straighten me. It's too late. I've grown this way because of your neglect, and I will not bend."

"Finally in desperation I took my saw and cut off the great heavy branch on the west side. The saw left an ugly scar, more than eight inches across. I stepped back and surveyed what I had done. I had cut off the major part of the tree, leaving only one branch growing skyward.

"More than half a century has passed since I planted that tree. My daughter and her family live there now. The other day I looked again at the tree. It is large. Its shape is better. It is a great asset to the home. But how serious was the trauma of its youth and how brutal the treatment I used to straighten it.

"When it was first planted, a piece of string would have held it in place against the forces of the wind. I could have and should have supplied that string with ever so little effort. But I did not, and it bent to the forces that came against it.

"I have seen a similar thing, many times, in children whose lives I have observed. The parents who brought them into the world seem almost to have abdicated their responsibility. The results have been tragic. A few simple anchors would have given them the strength to withstand the forces that have shaped their lives. Now it appears it is too late." (Gordon B. Hinckley, "Bring Up a Child in the Way He Should Go," *Ensign*, Nov. 1993, 54)

Be Consistent

"My mother was ever consistent. There were no surprises. If you disobeyed, you knew you'd reap the assigned consequences. When it comes to her devotion to God, she is ever faithful, ever true. My mother saw that we were in church ever Sunday. Only on rare occasions, in cases of definite illness, did we miss a Sunday. She taught consistency and faithfulness by example. Although one could hardly say I am consistent in raising my children, at least her consistency in her devotion to God has worked its way deep into my mind. " (Marnie Pehrson)

faithful devotion

"And let us not be weary in well doing: for in due season we shall reap, if we faint not."

-- *Galatians 6:9*

Accountable to Others and to God

"Fathers. Yours is the basic and inescapable responsibility to stand as the head of the family. That does not carry with it any implication of dictatorship or unrighteous dominion. It carries with it a mandate that fathers provide for the needs of their families. Those needs are more than food, clothing, and shelter. Those needs include righteous direction and the teaching, by example as well as precept, of basic principles of honesty, integrity, service, respect for the rights of others, and an understanding that we are accountable for that which we do in this life, not only to one another but also to the God of heaven, who is our Eternal Father." (Gordon B. Hinckley, "Bring Up a Child in the Way He Should Go," *Ensign*, Nov. 1993, 54)

precept & example

Foster Independence

"My father had a habit of asking questions of us children. He'd ask me, 'Marnie, would you rather be the smartest girl in school or the prettiest girl in school?' Whatever I said was ok, but whenever I gave the better answer, he'd say, 'You know, I think you're right. I think you're onto something there.' Our opinions were always valued and never belittled – even if they weren't exactly what he wanted to hear. But he always subtly reinforced the opinions we had that were sound and worthwhile. My father truly believes that children are smarter than most adults are. He honestly valued our opinions. This kind of unconditional respect enabled me to think for myself. I had literally no desire to conform to the crowd as a child or teenager. I virtually did not even know the meaning of the term 'peer pressure.' This gift of independent thinking allowed me to stand up for what was right even when it may have been unpopular. " (Marnie Pehrson)

power of questions

Open Conversations

Teach children values
by talking to them
"about one's values in
an open and natural
manner. Even more
important than *what* is
said, is *how* it is said.
This is because *how*
something is said can
create defenses and
resentment in children if it is said in a
lecture or scolding tone and style. Children
will be more receptive to a parent's values
if they are offered in everyday normal
conversation, while driving the car or
watching television or reading a book. This
last part refers to *when* a parent talks to
their children. After the fact is often too
late. Parents need to talk to their children
before it happens in a preventive way.

"An area of difficulty for many parents
is not knowing how to talk to their children
openly or having children brush their

it's how you say it

comments on values as trivial or silly. This is often true of older children who are embarrassed by such conversation or don't trust their parents to really communicate in an open manner based on past experiences. If parents have unfairly lectured or acted judgmental of children when they expressed opposite opinions, they will be hesitant to have an 'open conversation' with their parents. Only with patience, on the part of the parent, and testing, on the part of the child, will trust be renewed and values discussed." (Ron Huxley, LMFT, "Four Steps to Teaching Children Values", www.parentingtoolbox.com)

No Greater Blessing,
No Greater Mission

"Let every mother realize that she has no
greater blessing than the children which
have come to her as a gift from the
Almighty; that she has no greater mission
than to rear them in light and truth, in
understanding and love; that she will have
no greater happiness than to see them grow
into young men and women who respect
principles of virtue, who walk free from the
stain of immorality and from the shame of
delinquency." (Gordon B. Hinckley, "Bring
Up a Child in the Way He Should Go,"
Ensign, Nov. 1993, 54)

light and truth

Trust Your Children

"My parents trusted us implicitly. If we
were out at night, they only asked that we
call in if we were going to be late so that
they wouldn't worry that we had been in a
car wreck. They trusted us to do the right
thing, and because we knew they trusted
us, we would never want to let them down.
In contrast, I had friends whose parents let
them know that they did not trust them.
Invariably these friends proved themselves
untrustworthy." (Marnie Pehrson)

cherish trust

Society Only As Sound as Its Homes

"The health of any society, the happiness of its people, their prosperity, and their peace all find their roots in the teaching of children by fathers and mothers.

"The very structure of our society is now threatened by broken homes and the tragic consequences of those homes.

"I believe that with effort we can change this course. We must begin with parents. We must provide understanding on the part of every man and woman of the eternal purposes of life, of the obligations of marriage, and of the responsibilities of parenthood. To men who beget children and then abandon them, I say that God will hold you accountable, for these are also His children, whose cries over what you have done reach up to Him. With the obligation to beget goes the responsibility to nurture, to protect, to teach, to guide in righteousness and truth. Yours is the power and the responsibility to preside in a home where there is peace and security, love and harmony." (Gordon B. Hinckley, "Bring Up a Child in the Way He Should Go," *Ensign*, Nov. 1993, 54)

How Well Have My Children Done?

"You have nothing in this world more precious than your children. When you grow old, when your hair turns white and your body grows weary, when you are prone to sit in a rocker and meditate on the things of your life, nothing will be so important as the question of how your children have turned out. It will not be the money you have made. It will not be the cars you have owned. It will not be the large house in which you live. The searing question that will cross your mind again and again will be, How well have my children done?

"If the answer is that they have done very well, then your happiness will be complete. If they have done less than well, then no other satisfaction can compensate for your loss.

"And so I plead with you, my dear sisters. Sit down and quietly count the

searing question

debits and the credits in your role as a mother. It is not too late. When all else fails, there is prayer and the promised help of the Lord to assist you in your trials. But do not delay. Start now, whether your child be six or 16." (Gordon B. Hinckley, "Your Greatest Challenge, Mother," October 2000)

Who Can Measure A Mother's Love?

"One summer day I stood alone in the quiet of the American War Memorial Cemetery of the Philippines. A spirit of reverence filled the warm tropical air. Situated amidst the carefully mowed grass, acre upon acre, were markers identifying men, mostly young, who in battle gave their lives. As I let my eyes pass name by name along the many colonnades of honor, tears came easily and without embarrassment. As my eyes filled with tears, my heart swelled with pride. I contemplated the high price of liberty and the costly sacrifice many had been called upon to bear.

"My thoughts turned from those who bravely served and gallantly died. There came to mind the grief-stricken mother of each fallen man as she held in her hand the news of her precious son's supreme sacrifice. Who can measure a mother's grief? Who can probe a mother's love? Who can comprehend in its entirety the lofty role of a mother? With perfect trust in God, she walks, her hand in His, into the valley of the shadow of death, that you and I might come forth into light." (Thomas S. Monson, "Behold Thy Mother," *Liahona*, Apr. 1998, 2)

Mother Brings Out the Best in Men

"Men turn from evil and yield to their better natures when mother is remembered. A famed officer from the Civil War period, Colonel Higginson, when asked to name the incident of the Civil War that he considered the most remarkable for bravery, said that there was in his regiment a man whom everybody liked, a man who was brave and noble, who was pure in his daily life, absolutely free from dissipations in which most of the other men indulged.

"One night at a champagne supper, when many were becoming intoxicated, someone in jest called for a toast from this young man. Colonel Higginson said that he arose, pale but with perfect self-control, and declared: 'Gentlemen, I will give you a toast which you may drink as you will, but which I will drink in water. The toast that I have to give is, 'Our mothers.' '

"Instantly a strange spell seemed to come over all the tipsy men. They drank the toast in silence. There was no more

mother remembered

laughter, no more song, and one by one they left the room. The lamp of memory had begun to burn, and the name of Mother touched every man's heart." (Thomas S. Monson, "Behold Thy Mother," *Liahona*, Apr. 1998, 2)

"And all thy children shall be taught of the LORD; and great shall be the peace of thy children.

In righteousness shalt thou be established: thou shalt be far from oppression; for thou shalt not fear: and from terror; for it shall not come near thee."

- Isaiah 54:13-14

Behold thy Mother!

"The holy scriptures, the pages of history, are replete with tender, moving, convincing accounts of 'mother loved.' One, however, stands out supreme, above and beyond any other. The place is Jerusalem, the period known as the meridian of time. Assembled is a throng of Roman soldiers. Their helmets signify their loyalty to Caesar, their shields bear his emblem, their spears are crowned by Roman eagles. Assembled also are natives to the land of Jerusalem. Faded into the still night, and gone forever, are the militant and rowdy cries, 'Crucify him, crucify him.'

"The hour has come. The personal earthly ministry of the Son of God moves swiftly to its dramatic conclusion. A certain loneliness is here. Nowhere to be found are the lame beggars who, because of this man, walk; the deaf who, because of this man, hear; the blind who, because of this man, see; the dead who, because of this man, live.

mother loved

"There remained yet a few faithful followers. From his tortured position on the cruel cross he sees his mother and the disciple whom he loved standing by. He speaks: 'Woman, behold thy son! Then saith he to the disciple, Behold thy mother!' (John 19:26-27)

"From that awful hour when time stood still, when the earth did quake and great mountains were brought down—yes, through the annals of history, over the centuries of years and beyond the span of time—there echoes His simple yet divine words, 'Behold thy mother.'" (Thomas S. Monson, "Behold Thy Mother," *Liahona*, Apr. 1998, 2)

Seizing the Teaching Moment

Harold B. Lee once told of a mother who was polishing pieces of silver in preparation for a reception in the evening. "Right in the midst of all her preparations, her little eight year old boy came in with his piggy bank and he said to his mother, 'Mother, how do you pay your tithing?'

"And now of all times that she did not want to be interrupted, this was that time, but she wiped her hands and she sat down and they shook the pennies and the nickels and dimes out of the piggy bank and then she explained how he paid tithing. When she had finished, he threw his arms around her neck and said, 'Oh, thank you, Mother, for helping me; now I know how to pay my tithing.' "

"Commenting about the experience, the mother said something that is very, very important for all ... mothers to remember, 'Well, all my life I will have time to polish silver, but this may be the only time I will ever have to teach my boy the principle of tithing.' " (Harold B. Lee, In Conference Report, Mexico and Central America Area Conference 1972, 91.)

Endowed with Spiritual Gifts

"Woman's influence can bless a community or a nation to that extent to which she develops her spiritual powers in harmony with the heaven-sent gifts with which she has been endowed by nature. ... Year in and year out, she may cast the aura of her calming and refining influence to make certain that her posterity will enjoy the opportunities to develop to their fullest potential their spiritual and physical natures." (Harold B. Lee, *Ye Are the Light of the World,* 318-19.)

harmony with heaven

Creators of Home's Atmosphere

"Mothers are the creators of the atmosphere in the home and do much to provide the strong foundation for their sons and daughters, to provide them with strength when they leave the influence of their homes." (*The Teachings of Harold B. Lee,* 289.)

"We as women are the thermostats of the home. If I am stressed or my emotions are on edge, the children sense my state and reflect it in their own actions. The baby cries, the toddler whines, the kindergartner pitches tantrums and the teenager's emotions erupt. But if I am calm, serene and have taken time to sup from the pages of God's word, life is more peaceful. The baby rests, the toddler plays with the kindergartner and the teenager smiles and chats. It is amazing how one person can make or break the entire spirit of a home. What power, influence and responsibility a mother holds!" (Marnie Pehrson)

thermostat of home

Slow Down & Tune into Intuition

"Today I feel that women are becoming victims of the speed of modern living. It is in building their motherly intuition and that marvelous closeness with their children that they are enabled to tune in upon the wavelengths of their children and to pick up the first signs of difficulty, of danger and distress, which if caught in time would save them from disaster. " (*The Teachings of Harold B. Lee,* 288.)

"I say to you mothers, if you ever have sons and daughters who amount to what they should in the world, it will be in no small degree due to the fact that your children have a mother who spends many nights on her knees in prayer, praying God that her son, her daughter, will not fail. I remember at the foolish years of my teenage life, my mother came to me with an intuitive impression and warning which I brushed off as foolish teenagers do. "Oh, mother, that's silly," I said, then within only a month, to stand face to face with the

a mother on her knees

temptation about which mother had warned. I never had the courage to go back and tell her how right she was, but I was on guard because someone warned — my mother." (Harold B. Lee, "The Influence and Responsibility of Women," *Relief Society Magazine,* Feb. 1964, 85.)

"The ... fervent prayer of a righteous [parent] availeth much"

- James 5:16

God Speaks through Mother's Intuition

"A family consisting of my grandmother, my mother, and two or three of the younger children were seated before an open door, watching the great display of nature's fireworks as a severe thunderstorm raged near the mountain where our home was located. A flash of chain lightning followed by an immediate loud clap of thunder indicated that the lightning had struck very close.

"I was standing in the doorway when suddenly and without warning my mother gave me a vigorous push that sent me sprawling on my back out of the doorway. At that instant, a bolt of lightning came down the chimney of the kitchen stove, out through the open doorway, and split a huge gash from top to bottom in a large tree immediately in front of the house. If I had remained in the door opening, I wouldn't be writing this story today.

a mother warned

"My mother could never explain her split-second decision. All I know is that my life was spared because of her impulsive, intuitive action.

"Years later, when I saw the deep scar on that large tree at the old family home, I could only say from a grateful heart: Thank the Lord for that precious gift possessed in abundant measure by my own mother and by many other faithful mothers, through whom heaven can be very near in time of need." (*The Teachings of Harold B. Lee*, 290-91.)

A Mother's Heart is a Child's Schoolroom

"A mother's heart is a child's schoolroom. The instructions received at the mother's knee, and the parental lessons together with the pious and sweet souvenirs of the fireside, are never effaced entirely from the soul.

"Someone has said that the best school of discipline is the home, for family life is God's own method of training the young, and homes are largely what mothers make them." (*The Teachings of Harold B. Lee*, 289.)

Take Time to Teach

"Recently I came across a talk that had been
given by one of my daughters to a group of
mothers and daughters. She told an
experience with her first born son who
began to teach her the responsibilities that
she must have as a mother. She said, "Many
years ago when my oldest son was a very
little boy, I found myself one warm
summer night after supper frantically
trying to finish bottling some fruit." I am
sure you young mothers can picture that
scene. Everything had happened that day
to keep you from getting to that project and
you wanted to finish it. Now with the baby
settled for the night and your husband off
to his meeting on time, your little three and
four year olds are about finished getting
their pajamas and are getting ready for bed.
You think to yourself, "Well, now I will get
to that fruit."

"[My daughter continued:] 'This is the
situation I found myself in that night as I
began to peel and pit that fruit, when my
two little boys appeared in the kitchen and
announced that they were ready to say
their prayers.' But not wanting to be
interrupted, she said very quickly to her

boys, 'Now why don't you run in and say your prayers all alone and Mother will just keep on working at this fruit.' David, the oldest, planted his little feet firmly in front of me and asked, not unkindly, 'But, Mommy, which is the most important, the prayers or fruit?' Little did I realize then as a young mother and a busy wife that in my life ahead that there would be many such dilemmas as I carried out this role of wife and mother in my home.'

"That is the challenge that you as mothers have when your little children are pressing for you to stand by and help them grow. ...

"Mothers, when your children begin to ask you questions, even about the delicate things in life, don't turn them aside. Take time to explain to their childish minds, or as they grow up, to their older minds. A successful mother is one who is never too tired for her sons and daughters to come and share their joys and their sorrows with her." (Harold B. Lee, In Conference Report, Mexico and Central America Area Conference 1972, 90-91; paragraphing added.)

A Mother's Sacrifice

There are some lines attributed to Victor Hugo which read:

"She broke the bread into two fragments and gave them to her children, who ate with eagerness. 'She hath kept none for herself,' grumbled the sergeant.

" 'Because she is not hungry,' said a soldier.

" 'No,' said the sergeant, 'because she is a mother.' "

she is a mother

Claim the Promises

"When you have come to the Lord in meekness and lowliness of heart and, as one mother said, 'pounded on the doors of heaven to ask for, to plead for, to demand guidance and wisdom and help for this wondrous task,' that door is thrown open to provide you the influence and the help of all eternity. Claim the promises of the Savior of the world. Ask for the healing balm of the Atonement for whatever may be troubling you or your children. Know that in faith things will be made right in spite of you or, more correctly, because of you.

"You can't possibly do this alone, but you *do* have help. The Master of Heaven and Earth is there to bless you—He who resolutely goes after the lost sheep, sweeps thoroughly to find the lost coin, waits everlastingly for the return of the prodigal son. Yours is the work of salvation, and therefore you will be magnified, compensated, made more than you are and

doors of heaven

better than you have ever been as you try to make honest effort, however feeble you may sometimes feel that to be.

"Remember, remember all the days of your motherhood: 'Ye have not come thus far save it were by the word of Christ with unshaken faith in him, relying wholly upon the merits of him who is mighty to save.'" (From an address by Jeffrey R. Holland, *Ensign*, May 1997, 35-37).

Be at the Crossroads.

"Take time to always be at the crossroads when your children are either coming or going—when they leave and return from school, when they leave and return from dates, when they bring friends home. Be there at the crossroads whether your children are six or sixteen. In Proverbs we read, "A child left to himself bringeth his mother to shame" (Proverbs 29:15) (Ezra Taft Benson, Fireside given for parents, 22, February 1987)

be there

You may have tangible wealth untold;
Caskets of jewels and coffers of gold.
Richer than I you can never be —
I had a mother who read to me.

Strickland Gillilan,
"The Reading Mother."

read to your children

Love is the Foundation

"Is yours a culture where the husband exerts a domineering, authoritarian role, making all of the important decisions for the family? That pattern needs to be tempered so that both husband and wife act as equal partners, making decisions in unity for themselves and their family. No family can long endure under fear or force; that leads to contention and rebellion. Love is the foundation of a happy family" (Richard G. Scott, "Removing Barriers to Happiness," *Ensign,* May 1998, 86).

equal partners

Serve Others

"My mother has one of
those sixth senses about
serving other people. In the
morning I can use the last
of my fabric softener, and who is to turn up
on my doorstep that afternoon, but my
mother carrying a brand new bottle of
fabric softener. The woman is amazing. She
anticipates the needs and desires of her
children with the intuition of a psychic. She
lives to serve her children and others. "
(Marnie Pehrson)

nourish the spirit

Balance Between Love and Limits

"Too much love and a child becomes spoiled, expecting their every want and need to be met regardless of other peoples' wants and needs. This causes children to be stuck in those early stages of moral development based on selfish individualism. That's fine for a two-year-old, tolerable in a six-year-old, and obnoxious in a twelve-year-old or older. Too many limits and the child develop a low sense of worth and a lack of self-control. This usually results in an overly rebellious child or an unhealthy submissive one.

"Achieving this balance is difficult. But it is easier to do if discipline is viewed from the vantagepoint of moral development. We are not merely punishing wrong behavior. We are shaping character. We are not simply setting limits. We are teaching how to distinguish right from wrong. It is easier to say 'no' when I know that I am guiding my child's moral development and ultimately, his or her social success." (Ron Huxley, LMFT, *Moral Development of Children: Knowing Right and Wrong*, www.parentingtoolbox.com)

Family Night

"We are trying to preserve the traditional family — father, mother, and children — working together in love toward a common goal. In large measure we are succeeding against great odds. We advocate a family home evening, for instance, one night a week reserved for family activity together. Lessons from the scriptures are taught. Family business is discussed. Vacations are planned. We sing together. We pray together. It works!" (Gordon B. Hinckley, "Excerpts from Recent Addresses of President Gordon B. Hinckley," *Ensign,* Jan. 1998, 73-74).

it works!

Side by Side

"In the home it is a partnership with husband and wife equally yoked together, sharing in decisions, always working together. While the husband, the father, has responsibility to provide worthy and inspired leadership, his wife is neither behind him nor ahead of him but at his side." (Boyd K. Packer, "The Relief Society," *Ensign*, May 1998, 73).

equally yoked

"No other success in life can compensate for failure in the home."

-   David O. McKay

The Building Block of Society

Mrs. Margaret Thatcher, former Prime Minister of Great Britain, accurately observed: "The family is the building block of society. It is a nursery, a school, a hospital, a leisure center, a place of refuge and a place of rest. It encompasses the whole of the society. It fashions our beliefs; it is the preparation for the rest of our life." (Nicholas Wood, "Thatcher Champions the Family," *London Times*, 26 May 1988.)

a place of refuge

Family Prayer

"The old saying, 'The family that prays together stays together' is true. Nothing engenders more parental love for children than to watch your 2-year-old reverently bow his head, close his eyes and fold his arms as family prayers are said. Nothing builds more confidence in a child or teen than to hear her parents pray for her by name. Morning and evening family prayers bring a sense of unity and peace that is irreplaceable and unobtainable in any other way. It is a protection and a safeguard from the frightening world in which we live." (Marnie Pehrson)

unity and peace

The Hand that Rocks the Cradle

"Satan has declared war on motherhood. He knows that those who rock the cradle can rock his earthly empire. And he knows that without righteous mothers loving and leading the next generation, the kingdom of God will fail." (Sheri L. Dew, "Are We Not All Mothers?" *Ensign,* Nov. 2001, 96)

loving and leading

Family Scripture Study

"Studying the scriptures as a family develops a spirit of learning and love of God in the home. It's amazing how well children can learn to read when scriptures are regular read. Our four-year-old loves to take her turn to 'read' a verse during family scripture study. She really just repeats lines after her daddy reads them to her, but she never wants to miss her turn to 'read' along. This has also given her an increased interest in reading in general

"Reading scriptures together daily as a family builds faith in the Lord, an understanding of His attributes and His love for us. It promotes a sincere desire to follow His commandments. It also diminishes contention in the home. I've noticed a definite difference in the level of arguing in our home when we forget to read our scriptures regularly as a family versus when we remember to read them consistently.

spirit of learning

"It can be difficult working out schedules for everyone to read together, but it is worth it. If you have to, read in shifts to catch everyone. For example, to work around schedules, you may have to read with your older children before school and your younger ones at bedtime. It also takes some humor and patience – especially if you have children who like to goof off or little ones who can't sit still. We've found it's best not to take things so seriously, but to try to make it an enjoyable experience from which everyone can learn. " (Marnie Pehrson)

Who Are Your Child's Heroes?

"Heroes are another source of values. These are people, real or fictional, that are admired for certain characteristics they possess. Modeling is an important aspect of how children learn. Some theorist's feel that it is the most important variable for learning parental values (Bandura). Children will model their heroes or the people they most want to be like. These heroes could be celebrities, comic book heroes, teachers, relatives, friends, or one's parents.

"Television is often a reflection of what society as a whole considers to be parenting heroes. Over the years, models of family life have changed drastically. The parenting heroes of yesterday, the 'Ozzie and Harriet's' and the 'Father Knows Best,' have been replaced with the Cosby parents and Homer Simpson, not to mention numerous examples of single and step parent families. What society considers to be acceptable heroes or models of parents

influence values

have drastically changed. And the more similar the hero to the person, (i.e., same gender or race), the more influential that hero will be in the person's life. Children who observe parents "practicing what they preach" will be more likely to do these things as well. Seeing the positive effects parents experience as a result of living out their values and the negative effects that others experience as a result of not following certain values, will be even one of the most effective methods for teaching values. Remember that parents are already teaching children values, by their every action and their every word. The act of teaching values is not the most difficult part about parenting. Deciding what parents are teaching is the most difficult and important." (Ron Huxley, LMFT, "Old Fashioned Values in the Modern World", www.parentingtoolbox.com)

Create a Christ-Centered Home

"In a world such as ours where drugs are readily available, pornography is a mouse click away, and morally bereft entertainment pours into our homes, it's obvious that Satan is 'going to and fro in the earth, and walking up and down in it.' (Job 1:7) But we can take courage, even though we are encompassed about by Satan and his minions, 'for they that be with us are more than they that be with them' (2 Kings 6: 16). The Lord has given us guidance and direction on how to protect our families and ourselves.

"In Deuteronomy 6, before the children of Israel entered the Promised Land, which was filled with idol worshipping inhabitants, Moses gave them strict counsel. He warned them against forgetting the Lord and serving false idols (Deuteronomy 6:10-15).

"He told them to carry his words in their hearts (Deuteronomy 6:6) and to teach them diligently to their children. He told them to 'talk of them when thou sittest in thine house, and when thou walkest by the way, and when thou liest down, and when thou risest up' (Deuteronomy 6:7).

"Not only did he warn them that the prosperity of the Promised Land would tempt them to become proud and idolatrous (a natural outgrowth of forgetting the Lord), but also he gave them symbolic ways that they could remember God. He instituted 'frontlets' as a reminder. Frontlets were little strips of parchment rolled up and attached to bands of leather worn around the forehead or around the arm. They also put Moses' words on their gates and the posts of their homes. What rich symbolism!

"What if we did this today? I guess we might look kind of funny with scriptures strapped to our heads, but what about within our homes or even in our cars? If you were to post the admonition of Paul to seek 'whatsoever things are true...honest... just... pure... lovely... of good report... virtuous or praiseworthy' next to your TV set, how would that affect your choice of entertainment? (Philippians 4:8) If a picture of the Savior holding the little children graced the walls of your home, how would that affect the way you treated your little ones?

"Ezra Taft Benson said that people who are 'captained by Christ will be consumed in Christ… Enter their homes, and the pictures on their walls, the books on their shelves, the music in the air, their words and acts reveal them as Christians.' (Ezra Taft Benson, *Ensign*, Nov. 1985, 6-7)

"How would your children be affected if you took time to teach them as Moses suggested – when you sat in your homes, walked in the way (or drove in your cars), or when you lied down or rose up?

"How can you create a protective Christ-centered environment in your home? What books and magazines should you have in your home? What pictures and words can you hang on your walls? What music can you listen to? What verses can you memorize as a family to plant God's word deep within your heart? How can you systematically teach your children at all times and all places to serve the Lord?" (Marnie Pehrson)

Creating a Legacy of Faith

Henry B. Eyring gave the following guide for helping our families gain their own witness of the truthfulness of the gospel of Jesus Christ:

"Since it is the Holy Ghost who testifies of sacred truth, we can do at least three things to make that experience more likely for our families. First, we can teach some sacred truth. Then we can testify that we know what we have taught is true. And then we must act so that those who hear our testimony see that our actions conform with what we said was true. The Holy Ghost will then confirm to them the truth of what we said and that we knew it to be true.

"That is how a legacy of testimony is created, preserved, and transmitted in a family.... We must find other ways to convey our legacy of testimony, but the process of teaching, testifying, and living the truth will be the same...." (Henry B. Eyring, "A Legacy of Testimony,"April 1996; see *Ensign*, May 1996, p. 62)

Practice What You Preach

"Jesus did not give us license to break the commandments. He taught, 'Whosoever therefore shall break one of these least commandments, and shall teach men so, he shall be called the least in the kingdom of heaven: but whosoever shall do and teach them, the same shall be called great in the kingdom of heaven.' (Matthew 5:19)

"He taught the people that 'unless your righteousness shall exceed the righteousness of the scribes and the Pharisees, ye shall in no case enter into the kingdom of heaven.' (Matthew 5:20) On numerous occasions Jesus referred to the scribes and Pharisees as hypocrites. They strained at a gnat and let the camel pass through. They taught the letter of the law and completely missed the spirit of it. They did not practice or understand the spirit of what they taught.

"I find it interesting that Jesus combines doing with teaching. According to Him, those of us who teach, must also practice

children watch

what we preach. People learn from what
we do more than from what we say.
Children especially, watch our actions. You
can't slide anything past a child. For
example, if you tell a child it's wrong to
swear and then do it yourself, they'll call
you on it. There's no getting away with it.
It's integrity, congruency between talk and
action that Jesus is calling for here."
(Marnie Pehrson)

Lead, Don't Drive

"Many parents want children to blindly follow their teaching about values. They communicate to the child: 'do it my way or else' with no explanation on why it should be done that way. Consequently they do not take parents' values seriously. Some parents even try 'scare tactics' to frighten their children with negative news in the media or create horrible stories to keep their children away from harmful influences or behaviors. Although fear works, it is not the best method for teaching children values. This approach may result in traumatizing children emotionally

"Most importantly, parents must live the values they are trying to teach to their children. Children who observe parents 'practicing what they preach' will be more likely to do these things as well. Seeing the positive effects parents experience as a result of living out their values and the negative effects that others experience as a result of not following certain values, will be one of the most effective methods for

live your values

teaching values. Remember that parents are already teaching children values, by their every action and their every word. The act of teaching values is not the most difficult part about parenting. Deciding what parents are teaching is the most difficult and important." (Ron Huxley, LMFT, "Four Steps to Teaching Children Values",
www.parentingtoolbox.com)

Create Family Traditions

"Plan family activities, celebrate each other's birthdays, go to your children's sports events and musical recitals. Be there for your family during their triumphs. Create traditions in your family. In our family, we celebrate birthdays of aunts, uncles, and cousins with family dinners, cake and ice cream, and good association. In months where several people have birthday's, we often have one party to celebrate the combined birthdays.

"Giving your children the gift of friendships with their cousins, aunts and uncles is a priceless treasure. You are giving them happy memories and friendships that will last a lifetime and beyond.

"Another way to insure that your immediate family has enough activities is to set one night a week aside as a family night. On this night you can tell stories, read books, sing songs, plan activities, go to the movies or the mall together, and counsel with your spouse and children. It is a great way to build unity and love in your family. It insures that you have at least one evening a week as a family. Pick a night that fits all of your schedules, and stick with it. Set that night as an appointment that you will not break. " (Marnie Pehrson)

The Children's Hour
By: Henry Wadsworth Longfellow
(1807-1882)

*Between the dark and the daylight, When the
night is beginning to lower, Comes a pause in
the day's occupations, That is known as the
Children's Hour.*

*I hear in the chamber above me The patter of
little feet, The sound of a door that is opened,
And voices soft and sweet.*

*From my study I see in the lamplight,
Descending the broad hall stair, Grave Alice,
and laughing Allegra, And Edith with golden
hair.*

*A whisper, and then a silence: Yet I know by
their merry eyes They are plotting and planning
together To take me by surprise.*

*A sudden rush from the stairway, A sudden
raid from the hall! By three doors left
unguarded They enter my castle wall!*

patter of little feet

They climb up into my turret O'er the arms and back of my chair; If I try to escape, they surround me; They seem to be everywhere.

They almost devour me with kisses, Their arms about me entwine, Till I think of the Bishop of Bingen In his Mouse-Tower on the Rhine!

Do you think, O blue-eyed banditti, Because you have scaled the wall, Such an old mustache as I am Is not a match for you all!

I have you fast in my fortress, And will not let you depart, But put you down into the dungeon In the round-tower of my heart.

And there will I keep you forever, Yes, forever and a day, Till the walls shall crumble to ruin, And moulder in dust away!

Love, That You May Lead

"When I was growing up, it was not uncommon for Mother to wake me in the middle of the night and say, 'Sheri, take your pillow and go downstairs.' I knew what that meant. It meant a tornado was coming, and I was instantly afraid. But then Mother would say, 'Sheri, everything will be OK.' Her words always calmed me. Today, decades later, when life seems overwhelming or frightening, I call Mother and wait for her to say, 'Everything will be OK.'

"Recent horrifying events in the United States have underscored the fact that we live in a world of uncertainty. Never has there been a greater need for righteous mothers—mothers who bless their children with a sense of safety, security, and confidence about the future, mothers who teach their children where to find peace and truth and that the power of Jesus Christ is always stronger than the power of the adversary. Every time we build the

everything will be ok

faith or reinforce the nobility of a young
woman or man, every time we love or lead
anyone even one small step along the path,
we are true to our endowment and calling
as mothers and in the process we build the
kingdom of God. No woman who
understands the gospel would ever think
that any other work is more important or
would ever say, 'I am *just* a mother,' for
mothers heal the souls of men.

"Look around. Who needs you and your
influence? If we really want to make a
difference, it will happen as we mother
those we have borne and those we are
willing to bear with. If we will stay right
with our youth—meaning, if we will *love*
them—in most cases they will stay right
with us—meaning, they will let us *lead*
them." (Sheri L. Dew, "Are We Not All
Mothers?" *Ensign,* Nov. 2001, 96)

Author Index

www.ingramcontent.com/pod-product-compliance
Lightning Source LLC
Chambersburg PA
CBHW031320040426
42443CB00005B/158